THE *Faith* EXPERIMENT

LAUREL CHRISTENSEN

DESERET
BOOK

Salt Lake City, Utah

Library of Congress Cataloging-in-Publication Data
ISBN 978-1-60907-464-7
(CIP data on file)

Printed in the United States of America
R.R. Donnelley, Crawfordsville, IN

10   9   8   7   6   5   4   3   2   1

With love and gratitude to Tiffany Yeates Gust,
who, with the help of a treadmill,
helped me find the courage to see.

Contents

Journey of a Cheerful Pessimist

"Commit to something that feels beyond your reach."

That was the counsel I was given as I left a two-week experience at a fitness and health spa. The entire two weeks had already felt beyond my reach, but I had made a commitment to change my life and I was ready for the next step on the journey.

As I drove the highway back to my home, I passed a billboard advertising a half marathon through Provo Canyon in Provo, Utah. The date was six months away. And six months sounded like plenty of time for *anyone* to get ready for a half

Commit to something that feels

beyond your REACH.

marathon—even a girl like me who had yet to run a full mile.

When I arrived home, I told everyone I knew about my plan; I knew the peer pressure would be helpful and I was actually excited about the thought of doing something big. I created a training plan that would require me to stay on the path I had begun the previous two weeks.

Then, two months later, when I was still working my way up to running a full mile without dying, I had a back injury. It felt like such a big obstacle—the kind of obstacle that begins a spiraling downfall. I had a pattern of spiraling fast when something big and disappointing appeared to be in my way. A really good friend of mine was watching this happen, and she said, "Well, at least you're the most cheerful pessimist there ever was."

Honestly, when she said it, I was a little offended. My reaction was, "I'm not a pessi— oh, yes, yes, I am. I think I actually am a pessimist." I said to her, "You know, if I was a superhero, I would be

Worst-Case Scenario Girl. That is who I would be."
I had always been so good at going to "worst-case
scenario." It was a world I knew well. It was a world
I had become very comfortable with.

The truth is that I was generally really positive
and really happy and really believing. I believed in
happy endings (for other people). And I believed
that God would hear and answer prayers (for anyone
but me). And I absolutely believed that good things
happen (not as often as bad things, but good things
nonetheless).

But I also knew heartbreaking disappointment,
I knew that sometimes the answer is just "no," and I
knew that sometimes what we want just doesn't happen. And so I suppose, because I had experiences on
both sides, I had started to develop some thoughts
about my life—and, more seriously, some thoughts
about my Father in Heaven—that were neither accu-
rate nor healthy.

During those times when things started looking
like they weren't going right, I would start to panic

and retreat and my mind would go south . . . and go south quickly. It was almost as if I was setting myself up so that when things didn't work out—like I already knew they wouldn't—I could be okay. My faith could still be intact and my relationship with my Father in Heaven could be spared from damage.

The problem with that kind of behavior is that the very thing I thought was protecting my faith was actually weakening my faith.

So after a couple of weeks of playing Worst-Case Scenario Girl with my back injury, I knew I needed to do something to get myself back on track. I had only a couple of months before the half marathon and I was not about to let this big goal go by the wayside like so many others in my life had. I decided I needed to embark on some kind of an experiment that would help me in the faith department, and I started something I called "The Optimist Experiment"—an experiment in which I would commit to be optimistic and fight the tendency to go to "worst case" just because I hit an obstacle. I knew I needed to see my world differently. I knew I needed to see myself differently. But I wasn't entirely sure how to do it.

It was about that time that I heard a talk by Elder D. Todd Christofferson in general conference. He said, "Our Heavenly Father is a God of high expectations" ("'As Many as I Love,'" 97). That opening statement pricked my heart, and I don't know that I consciously heard anything else in his message. I heard those words and I immediately thought, "If that's true, then I wonder if I can have high expectations too."

What would happen if I continued on this journey not just asking for help from heaven but expecting it?

What would happen if I continued on this journey not just asking for help from heaven but expecting it? It wouldn't be easy for me, but I couldn't help but feel like it would make a significant difference.

I went to my scriptures, as I often do when I'm

Our Heavenly Father

is a God of

high expectations.

—ELDER D. TODD CHRISTOFFERSON

beginning something difficult, and I opened them to the book of Moroni. In Moroni 7:20, Mormon says, "And now, my brethren, how is it possible that ye can lay hold upon every good thing?" I love that question because a question in the scriptures is often followed by an answer, but I particularly loved that question at that moment because I knew that what I was trying to do was a good thing. Sure, it wasn't the most important thing on the planet. I wasn't trying to solve the Middle East crisis. I wasn't trying to fix the world economy. My losing weight and training for a half marathon wasn't the biggest deal in the world, but it was important to me. I knew it was a good thing. And I wanted to know how to "lay hold upon" it.

The answer to this great question is found a few verses later: "Wherefore, by the ministering of angels, and by every word which proceeded forth out of the mouth of God, men began to exercise faith in Christ; and *thus by faith, they did lay hold upon every good thing*" (Moroni 7:25; emphasis added).

I read that and thought, "Oh, if it's just a matter of faith, we're fine."

Well, here's my little confession: Of all the principles of the gospel, I would have to say that faith has been the hardest one for me—which has created a little bit of a problem, because it's the first principle, and if you struggle with the first principle, you're probably going to be in trouble on all the rest. I realized that optimism comes from faith, and so I changed the name of my experiment from "The Optimist Experiment" to "The Faith Experiment," with a commitment to do three things:

1. PRAY with faith
2. THINK with faith
3. LIVE with faith

And that's how the journey really began.

Pray with Faith

I don't know about you, but I had a "plan A" for my life. (Surely I am not the only girl who attempted to plan out her life.) I remember sitting around with some of my girlfriends one day when we were all in college. We were discussing my "plan A," and that led to "plan B" . . . which led me to think about "plan C." I sort of wrote out my life plans and realized that I was already on "plan K." (And this was a problem because I hadn't even served a mission yet. By the time I went on my mission, I was beyond "plan K.")

Several years later, after the mission, I was with

another group of friends, kind of going through the same thing, and by then I was on "plan W." It's safe to say I am now in the Greek alphabet somewhere, perhaps plan "kappa"?

I suppose because I had beliefs (hopes?) about some things that would happen in my life, when they didn't happen, I started to develop ideas that I now see were false—ideas about what Heavenly Father wanted or what He didn't want for my life, ideas about what I was worthy of having in my life. I really struggled with that concept and found myself developing a belief that, for whatever reason, God wasn't going to ever give me what I really wanted.

> I found myself developing a belief that, for whatever reason, God wasn't going to ever give me what I really wanted.

I would sit in church and hear the scripture that reads: "What man is there of you, whom if his son ask bread, will he give him a stone?" (Matthew 7:9). I found it odd that the scripture was stated in such a

What man is there of you,

whom if his son ask BREAD,

will he give him a stone?

—MATTHEW 7:9

way to express that the premise was ridiculous—because I didn't find it so ridiculous.

Instead, my little heart would want to say, "Why is that such an absurd question to ask? I actually feel like I've asked for bread plenty of times and received a stone. Pretty stones and perfectly nice stones . . . but stones nonetheless." And because I felt this way, I simply stopped asking. It was easier to not ask—to be His dutiful, obedient daughter who was content with what she had—than to ask and risk being disappointed by a sincere petition going unanswered yet again.

And so, when I found myself with a back injury shortly into my half-marathon training, I was desperate for some help and I couldn't bring myself to ask my Father in Heaven for it. I ended up at the home of a dear friend requesting a priesthood blessing. In the blessing, without knowing very much about how I felt—for sure without knowing how I felt about this particular scripture—he said, "Your

Father wants to give you bread when you ask for bread."

It was as if time stopped. I don't remember hearing anything else. And I found myself asking, "What if He does? What if He really wants to give me bread? And I just haven't asked?" I knew that day that if something was going to change in my life, particularly where faith was concerned, I had to be willing to ask for bread.

What if He really wants to give me bread? And I just haven't asked?

When you haven't asked for anything for a while, it can be a little scary to start up again. I couldn't handle the thought of setting myself up and determined that I couldn't just ask amiss. I knew that if I was asking for bread, it had better be the right kind of bread. So I went to my scriptures again. This time I ended up at 3 Nephi 18:20: "And whatsoever ye shall ask the Father in my name, *which is right,* believing that ye shall receive, behold it shall be given unto you" (emphasis added).

And whatsoever ye shall ask the

Father in my name, which is right,

believing that ye shall receive,

behold it shall be GIVEN unto you.

—3 NEPHI 18:20

The "which is right" phrase took me to the Doctrine and Covenants: "Behold, you have not understood; you have supposed that I would give it unto you, when you took no thought save it was to ask me. But, behold, I say unto you, that you must study it out in your mind; then you must ask me if it be right, and if it is right I shall cause that your bosom shall burn within you; therefore, you shall feel that it is right" (D&C 9:7–8).

> Instead of just asking for those things that I desire, or that I want most in my life, I first go to my Father and ask Him if it is right to ask for that thing.

After pondering that scripture, I knew that if I was going to ask for bread—especially if I was going to ask in faith—I had to know that it was okay to ask for this particular brand of bread. And that has become my pattern for prayer. Instead of just asking for those things that I desire, or that I want most in my life, I first go to my Father and ask Him if it is right to ask for that thing. All I can tell you is this:

ONCE

you know that the thing

you are praying for is

acceptable to God—

that it's an okay thing to

ask for—it completely

changes your ability to

pray with faith.

You might feel like I do. I've often felt like the widow in the widow's mite story. My faith seems so small and so insufficient. What I have learned is that as long as it is every little bit of faith I have to lay on that altar before the Lord, it is enough. He makes it enough every time.

Is there something your heart longs for? Is there something you want? Are you ready to ask Him? Are you willing to *start asking Him again?* Find out if it is right to pray for that and then have the courage to pray with faith.

Think with Faith

When I began the journey of losing weight and changing my physical life, I left my world behind for two weeks to do something completely drastic and immerse myself in an environment that would push my physical limits. And it. Was. Hard.

The spa staff gave us a warning during our orientation that we might feel like we wanted to die on the second day. I remember waking up that morning feeling pretty good and just telling myself all day, "I can do this." We spent six hours a day in cardio, took a hike every morning, and had a menu of 1200 calories. It was intense, and every day got a little harder.

By Thursday morning, I was worried I wouldn't be able to do much more. After returning from the hike, I found a quiet little place in the locker room to check my phone. I was hoping for a text or an email from one of my many friends who had offered support and prayers for this experience. One in particular caught my eye:

> "You gain strength, courage, and confidence by every experience in which you really stop to look fear in the face . . . do the thing you THINK you cannot do."
> —Eleanor Roosevelt

Little did I know how much I would need that quote in the very next class coming up.

That class was a high-intensity cardio interval class (see "BLR Featured Class: Treading"). This is how it works: They told us to choose our favorite cardiovascular machine. And I remember thinking,

YOU gain strength, courage, and confidence by *every experience* in which you really stop to look fear in the face . . . do the thing you THINK you cannot do.

—ELEANOR ROOSEVELT

"Really? People have a favorite cardiovascular machine? Oh, okay." Then we were to work on the machine in these time increments and intensities:

5 minute warm-up
5 minutes as hard as you can go
5 minute recovery
4 minutes as hard as you can go
4 minute recovery
3 minutes as hard as you can go
3 minute recovery
2 minutes as hard as you can go
2 minute recovery
1 minute as hard as you can go
1 minute recovery
5 minute cooldown

Our instructors told us to choose a speed that was "as hard as you can go." But that obviously means different things to different people, and I wasn't sure what that was for me. I asked one of the trainers. I wanted a number . . . something to shoot for. She said, "You know what it is."

And I did.

I had a speed on my treadmill that I had worked up to that would be considered a "light jog" by most people's standards. And even then it was a "five-minute-on, five-minute-off" kind of thing. I knew if I was really going to go "as hard as I could go," I needed to choose a speed higher than that number.

The problem was, I KNEW I could not do it. I didn't just think I couldn't—I knew, really truly knew, I could not. But in that class, I had a woman on either side of me, and we all decided that was the speed we would start the class at.

Two minutes into the first five-minute "as hard as you can go" interval, I knew I was in trouble. I got that feeling that, when I would feel it at home on my treadmill, I would slow down because I thought my heart was going to rupture. (And who wants to die on their treadmill alone?)

"I can't do it. I can't do it," I huffed out.

"Yes, you can, Laurel. You can do this," my treadmill buddies said back to me.

"I can't. I can't," I huffed back.

And that's when one of the trainers saw what was happening. She came over and stood in front of me.

"Don't you dare stop. You can do this. Don't be the thing standing in your way of finishing. Go. Go. Go. Go. Go!"

The timer on the treadmill was not moving fast enough, and I didn't know how I could finish. I found myself thinking of all the things I wanted in my life . . . all the things that seemed so out of reach . . . all the things I had told myself for so long could not be . . . that I wasn't worthy of . . . and I just wanted to stop.

I looked down. There was one minute left.

But I couldn't breathe, and I was scared. I was exhausted. And I really actually thought I might die.

"Thirty seconds!" Trainer Tiffany yelled. "Don't you dare stop!"

Then I heard her yell the numbers: "Ten . . . nine . . . eight . . . seven . . . six . . . five . . . four . . . three . . . two . . . ONE!"

Time was up. I hopped to the side of the treadmill and bent over to try to catch my breath, and I sobbed.

> Don't be the thing standing in your way of finishing.

A short five minutes earlier, I didn't just think I couldn't do those full five minutes—I KNEW I couldn't. I knew I was going to have to stop before it was time to stop. I KNEW it. And yet, here I was in the five-minute recovery, sobbing, trying to catch my breath, trying to grab some water, but I wasn't dead. I had done it.

Then it was time for the next interval—a four-minute interval.

"I really can't do this again. I really, really can't," I said out loud between gasping for breaths.

"Yes, you can, Laurel. You can do this," my treadmill buddies said again.

"Get ready to increase your speed," Tiffany yelled.

And we got to the speed again. And again, I thought I was going to die. And again, Tiffany saw what was happening. And once again, she came over and stood right in front of my treadmill.

"You know you want this. Don't doubt your ability to get it done. Don't be the one thing standing in your way. You have this, Laurel. You have this!"

I thought of all those things again—all those things I had always wanted for myself. The sobbing started sometime during the last minute. Breathing is hard enough without sobbing, and that was when I knew I had to stop.

I was getting ready to jump off to the side, but something in me kept going. And the next thing I knew, I heard: "Thirty seconds!" Trainer Tiffany yelled. "Don't you dare stop!"

Then "Ten . . . nine . . . eight . . . seven . . . six . . . five . . . four . . . three . . . two . . . ONE! Recover."

My mind was spinning. I had done something I KNEW I could not do . . . not just once but twice.

And that meant only one thing: I. Was. Wrong.

I didn't even have time to process it when it was time for the three-minute interval. And I thought if I could do the speed I previously could not do for five and four minutes, maybe I could go faster for three.

> I had done something I KNEW I could not do . . . not just once but twice. And that meant only one thing: I. Was. Wrong.

And then the cycle started again:

Me thinking I couldn't.

People yelling at me that I could.

The ten-second countdown.

Me crying at the side of the treadmill.

And the speed climbed again every interval.

And I kept going until the end of the time.

I cried throughout the entire cooldown. I looked to my right and my left. "Thank you," I quietly whispered to my treadmill buddies. The trainer came over and simply said, "Don't you EVER forget what you just did."

Something happens when you do the thing you think you cannot do. Mrs. Roosevelt was right. You DO gain strength, courage, and confidence. But you also gain SOMETHING ELSE.

When I stepped off that treadmill, I had the "aha" of a lifetime. I realized I was not who I thought I was. I had walked into that class with limits on my abilities and limited ideas about what my life was supposed to be like . . . what it COULD be like. And, well, if the limits I thought I had were wrong, the limited ideas about what my life was supposed to be like or could be like were probably wrong too.

I had been standing in my own way. Or rather, the thoughts I had about my life—my faithless way of thinking—had been getting in the way of my living the life I was meant to live.

That is no small thing.

One of my favorite scriptures is in Ephesians 3:20. It describes our Father in Heaven as "him who is able to do exceeding abundantly above all that we ask or think." Don't you love that? It doesn't say "a little bit more" than we asked for. It says "exceeding abundantly above." I realized that while I can ask an inch for my life, He can and does think about

HIM who is able to do
exceeding abundantly above
all that we ask or think.

—EPHESIANS 3:20

hundreds of feet for me. And I knew that day I could never, ever, EVER think about myself or my life the same way again. That is the power of thinking with faith.

I gained an entirely new view of myself on that treadmill that day and I walked out of that class knowing I could never be the same again. Because the girl I thought I was simply didn't exist anymore. I became the girl who does the thing I think I cannot do.

What about you?

What's the thing you think you cannot do?

Don't be the one thing standing in your way.

Live with Faith

In his April 2011 general conference talk, Elder Dallin H. Oaks said, "When we have a vision of what we can become, our desire and our power to act increase enormously" ("Desire," 44). We must have a view of the life God has waiting for us in order to live that life with faith.

One of my favorite scripture stories is the story of Joseph of Egypt. Oh, how I love this story! I think it is fascinating because at age seventeen, Joseph literally had a vision of who and what he could become. It was very clear to him that his life was meant to be something unique and that he was

*W*hen we have a *vision*
of what we can BECOME, our
desire and our power to act
increase enormously.

—ELDER DALLIN H. OAKS

meant for something special. And, perhaps because he got a little overzealous, his brothers got a little tired of him telling the story over and over again. To make a long story short, they end up putting him in the pit (which was better than the alternative because a couple of them thought they should just kill him). I don't know about you, but if I were Joseph of Egypt at that moment and I had been thrown in the pit, I'm pretty sure Worst-Case Scenario Girl would have kicked right in.

I probably would have said something like, "Hmmm. Isn't this interesting? I totally thought I was meant for something really special. Now here I am in this pit. So, I guess I'll just stay in the pit and I won't ask to get out of the pit because if God didn't want me in the pit, He wouldn't have put me in the pit in the first place. Yes, I'll just stay right here and be the best girl there ever was in a pit until He chooses to get me out of it."

Then, as if that weren't enough for Joseph, after the pit, these same brothers sell him into slavery.

I don't about you, but Worst-Case Scenario Girl would have said something like, "Well, would you look at this! Now I'm a slave. I didn't even ask to get out of the pit. This is nice. I'm not really sure what I'm supposed to do as a slave, but I'm certainly not going to ask because I didn't ask the first time, and look where that got me. So we're just going to stay here and be the best slave there ever was."

And then, as if that weren't enough, Joseph ends up in jail. I don't know about you, but that would *not* have been Worst-Case Scenario Girl for me. That would have been an abandonment of everything I thought I knew about God. I am quite certain I would have been completely convinced that my early vision was made up or completely misunderstood or clearly intended for somebody else.

Joseph, on the other hand? He seems never to have lost sight of his understanding of what he was meant to do and who he was meant to be. Why? Go read Genesis 37 and 39–41 (you can skip the "genealogy" of 38), and underline how many times it says, "The Lord was with him."

Joseph was given a vision. He never gave up on that vision of who he could become *because the Lord was with him.* The Lord was with him in the pit, when he couldn't see a way out. The Lord was with him as a slave, when he felt he was in bondage to whatever it was that was holding him back. The Lord was with him in the jail, when he felt like he was in a box he couldn't get out of on his own.

As I read that story, I am reminded of all the times the Lord has been with me. He's been with me in the pits of my life. He's been with me when I felt like a slave to old thoughts or old habits or old patterns. And He's been with me when I was in jail and felt trapped by the confines I had put on myself.

We have been taught that to truly exercise the power of faith in our lives, we need to have three things. The first is the knowledge that God exists. The second is a correct understanding of His attributes. The third is that the course of life we are pursuing is acceptable to Him (see *Lectures on Faith,* 38).

One of my least favorite phrases is "Today is the first day of the rest of my life." I think I used to have it on a refrigerator magnet. But I don't like that phrase anymore because I feel like it discounts all the other days that got me right where I am. I used to be the queen of fresh starts—and, true confession, I still am. I like knowing that I have a new day to begin. I love getting a new journal and "starting today." But a fresh start should not come at the expense of acknowledging all the other days that got me here. We are all a product of all of our "other days."

It took me a long time to realize I'm not on plan K. I'm not on plan W. I'm not on plan Kappa.

I'm on plan A.

I just didn't know this was my plan A.

But I love where I am because this was *His* plan A for me. Where I am is no surprise to God. Where you are today is no surprise to your Father in Heaven. You're not further ahead than He thought you'd be.

You're not way back behind where He thought you'd be. You're right where He knew you would be.

Now, that doesn't mean He would have wished any of the difficult things in your life upon you; it's that He knew this would be your plan A. And once we know we are living our plan A, it completely changes our ability to live with faith.

I spent way too much of my life having faith in an outcome. Then, when the outcome didn't happen, I thought it was a commentary on my faith. The importance of faith is that it's centered in Jesus Christ—that regardless of the outcome, your faith can still be intact because you trust Him and you trust His power and you trust His mercy and you trust His grace. I also spent too much of my life confused about hope and faith and the difference between those two things.

This is what I've learned about hope and faith:

Hope is about wanting what *I* want. And it's okay to want things and to have desires and to hope for those things.

Faith is about wanting what GOD wants

for you. That's not faith in an outcome,

it's faith in His plan for you—your plan A.

LIVE WITH FAITH.

The Experiment

I committed to pray with faith and to think with faith and to live with faith in the hopes that it would get me to the finish line of that half marathon. And the obstacles came. And the injuries came. Several of them, in fact.

But I, Laurel Christensen, on June 11, 2011, completed the Utah Valley Half Marathon.

It was, I think, the hardest thing I've ever done. And even after all the "faith talk" and the whole experiment, I almost didn't finish.

I had done this hard thing in my training for months. And I was there at the race, and I was

committed. Then, about six and half miles in, I got a cramp in my left calf. I had been running the whole time without stopping. I hadn't been able to run quite that far in my training without having difficulty. So when the cramp came, I felt defeated. I remember thinking that it might be over. (Worst-Case Scenario Girl, anyone?) But I also had a lot of pride. I knew there were people waiting for me at certain mile markers. I knew I needed to keep going. There was one moment right past mile twelve, probably at about mile twelve and a half. I was looking down, and I knew that I was getting close to the finish line. A friend of mine who had started the race that morning and had finished much earlier came back to run with me.

By then I was mostly walking and feeling defeated (and I might have been crying . . . I might have been). I just wanted to quit. As we got to that point, probably a few hundred yards ahead, I could see the arch that said *FINISH*. I remember thinking, "Isn't that nice? That just looks so pretty. But I don't need to go. I'm just going to quit." And I said to my friend, "I need to be done."

He responded with, "Seriously? You're just going to quit? Do you see how close you are?" And I saw. But I had the T-shirt and I had done this really amazing thing and did I really need a medal to prove that I had already done more than anyone (including me) would have thought I could do? Honestly, I hurt in places I didn't know I had. So at that point, I just thought, "We have done everything we needed to do. I have nothing to prove anymore. I did what I needed to do."

> Did I really need a medal to prove that I had already done more than anyone (including me) would have thought I could do?

At that point, the course takes you through the barricade area where people are lined up. Hundreds of people were cheering. (I'm pretty sure there was probably a crowd of people who thought, "Oh, that woman is going to die. We should at least cheer for her as she comes in.") And then I heard my name. "Go, Laurel! Go, Laurel!" I looked over, and I saw two little boys with posters that said "You can do it" and "Go, Laurel!"

But I did not know those two little boys. They were the grandsons of a sweet woman who reads my blog. She was there supporting her husband, who was also running the race, and she had her grandsons hold these signs up for me. Now, when you're running and you think you're going to die, you for sure don't want to die in front of two cute boys. And hearing them saying my name and cheering me on? Well, I had no choice but to keep going. And I finished my first half marathon.

But it is fascinating to me that, at mile 12.5, even when I could see the finish line, I was willing and ready to quit.

Elder Jeffrey R. Holland, in a masterful address at BYU in 1999, said this:

YES, there are cautions and considerations to make,

but once there has been genuine illumination, beware the temptation to retreat from a *good thing*. If it was right when you prayed about it and trusted it and lived for it, it is right now. Don't give up when the pressure mounts. . . . Don't give in.

Certainly don't give in to that being who is bent on the destruction of your happiness. He wants everyone to be miserable like unto himself. Face your doubts. *Master your fears. 'Cast not away therefore your confidence.' Stay the course and see the* beauty of life *unfold for you."* ("'Cast Not Away Therefore Your Confidence,'" March 2, 1999)

Consider the possibility that God sees the potential for your life in a way that you have not seen yet—or are afraid to see. He is standing by, ready for you to believe that all things are possible—all right and worthy things are possible—for your life. He is ready for you to choose to become the person He has always known you to be. You are living your plan A. And the rest of the plan He has for you—has always been preparing for you—is ready to unfold before you as you pray with faith, as you think with faith, as you live with faith.

Are YOU ready

to try your own

faith experiment?

Don't be the ONE THING

standing in your way.

Sources

"BLR Featured Class: Treading." Accessed online at http:// www.biggestloserresort.com/blog/entry/blr-featured -class-treading

Christofferson, D. Todd. "'As Many as I Love, I Rebuke and Chasten.'" *Ensign,* May 2011, 97–100.

Holland, Jeffrey R. "'Cast Not Away Therefore Your Confidence.'" BYU Devotional, March 2, 1999, accessed online at http://speeches.byu.edu/?act=viewitem&id=795.

Lectures on Faith. Salt Lake City: Deseret Book, 1985.

Oaks, Dallin H. "Desire." *Ensign,* May 2011, 42–45.